Leading the Dillinger Gang: The Lives and Legacies of John Dillinger and Baby Face Nelson

By Charles River Editors

About Charles River Editors

Charles River Editors was founded by Harvard and MIT alumni to provide superior editing and original writing services, with the expertise to create digital content for publishers across a vast range of subject matter. In addition to providing original digital content for third party publishers, Charles River Editors republishes civilization's greatest literary works, bringing them to a new generation via ebooks.

Introduction

John Dillinger (1903-1934)

"I will be the meanest bastard you ever saw when I get out of here." – John Dillinger

America has always preferred heroes who weren't clean cut, an informal ode to the rugged individualism and pioneering spirit that defined the nation in previous centuries. The early 19th century saw the glorification of frontier folk heroes like Davy Crockett and Daniel Boone. After the Civil War, the outlaws of the West were more popular than the marshals, with Jesse James and Billy the Kid finding their way into dime novels. And at the height of the Great Depression in the 1930s, there were the "public enemies", common criminals and cold blooded murderers elevated to the level of folk heroes by a public frustrated with their own inability to make a living honestly.

Two months after Franklin D. Roosevelt's inauguration in 1933, a petty thief who had spent almost a decade behind bars for attempted theft and aggravated assault was released from jail. By the end of the year, that man, John Dillinger, would be America's most famous outlaw: Public Enemy Number One. From the time of his first documented heist in early July 1933, until his dramatic death in late July of the following year, he would capture the nation's attention and imagination as had no other outlaw since Jesse James.

His exploits were real, and in many cases impressive, but Dillinger's importance and legacy have always been partly symbolic. The country was in a panic over a supposed crime wave that some historians believe was more perception than reality, but a new breed of criminal targeting the nation's already vulnerable banks was a potent illustration and metaphor of the way society's institutions and morals seemed to be coming undone. And in the mind of the public, the outlaws of the 30s were very different from the gangsters of the 20s; they hailed from the farm country of America's nostalgic past, not the corrupt cities of its unsettled present and scarier future. Much was made of Dillinger's roots in the farming town of Mooresville, Indiana, even though he came of age in Indianapolis, and was very much a city boy at heart.

Ultimately, the story of Dillinger and the era's other famous criminals—Bonnie and Clyde, Baby Face Nelson, Pretty Boy Floyd—would largely be seen as a story of America's fall from grace. Just before Dillinger was released from prison in 1933, a feature article ran entitled "The Farmer Turned Gangster." America saw in Dillinger what it wanted to see, and even in Dillinger's lifetime it was nearly impossible to separate myth from reality.

Even still, Dillinger would never have become the mythical figure he became if J. Edgar Hoover and the FBI hadn't actively marketed him as "Public Enemy Number One," and if he hadn't died in a way that was almost scripted for Hollywood. Dillinger's figure looms so large in American history and popular culture that it's easy to forget that his starring role in the daily news lasted for less than a year.

Leading the Dillinger Gang looks at the life and crime of the famous outlaw, but it also humanizes him and analyzes his lasting legacy. Along with pictures of Dillinger and important people, places, and events in his life, you will learn about the infamous public enemy like you never have before, in no time at all.

Baby Face Nelson (1908-1934)

"He had a baby face. He was good looking, hardly more than a boy, had dark hair and was wearing a gray topcoat and a brown felt hat, turned down brim." –The wife of Chicago Mayor Big Bill Thompson describing the man who attacked her and stole her jewelry in October 1930.

The man who became Public Enemy Number One after the deaths of John Dillinger and Pretty Boy Floyd was Lester Joseph Gillis, whose alias "George Nelson" eventually gave way to the nickname "Baby Face Nelson". Despite the almost playfully innocent nickname, and the fact that he was not as notorious as two of his partners in crime, Dillinger and Floyd, Baby Face Nelson was the worst of them all.

In an era where the outlaws were glorified as Robin Hood types, Baby Face was a merciless outlier who pulled triggers almost as fast as he lost his temper. By the time fate caught up with Baby Face Nelson in November 1934 at the "Battle of Barrington", a shootout that left his body riddled with nearly 20 bullet holes, he was believed to have been responsible for the deaths of more FBI agents than anybody else in American history. It was a distinction he would have appreciated; during one bank robbery, Baby Face Nelson gleefully screamed "I got one!" after shooting police officer Hale Keith several times.

Due to his association with Dillinger and his own crime spree, Baby Face Nelson became a fixture of pop culture and was the main character in a few Hollywood films two decades after his death. Though he is not remembered as colorfully as Dillinger or Bonnie and Clyde, he is often remembered paradoxically as being a devoted family man who even had his wife and children on the run with him.

Leading the Dillinger Gang looks at the life and crime of the famous outlaw, but it also humanizes him and examines his lasting legacy. Along with pictures of Baby Face Nelson and important people, places, and events in his life, you will learn about the infamous public enemy like you never have before, in no time at all.

Baby Face Nelson's Wanted Poster

Chapter 1: The Times

The United States of the 1920s was a time and place of tremendous contradiction. Called "The Roaring Twenties" by some and the "Jazz Age" by others, it has been romanticized as a carefree era of speakeasies, flapper girls, jazz and moonshine. This is part truth and part myth, an image cultivated even at the time by the likes of F. Scott Fitzgerald in his novel *The Great Gatsby*. But it was one of the great conservative social experiments of American history, the 18th Amendment prohibiting the sale of alcohol, that set the stage for the gaiety and casual lawlessness that prevailed during the decade.

Politically, it was a conservative era characterized by a retreat from political reform and internationalism. Disillusioned by the nation's late but expensive entry into World War I, Americans seemed to turn inward toward private pleasures and private concerns. The Red Scare that had flared briefly during the war was followed by an ongoing backlash against immigrants that found expression in the imposition of strict immigration quotas, and in the revival of the Ku Klux Klan. The passion of the Progressive Era for social reform was replaced by a concern with prosperity. As President Calvin Coolidge famously said at the time, "The chief business of the American people is business."

The Chicago gangster Al Capone was both an icon and a kind of folk hero of the era. Though he attained great wealth through a host of illegal activities that included saloons, brothels, and whiskey running, he tried to create an image of himself as just another successful businessman. He was part of a new breed of organized crime figures that ran their outfits like corporations and were part of regional and even national networks. The evolution of modern law enforcement to keep up with their increasingly sophisticated ways would be echoed in the '30s by the emergence of the modern FBI in response to the crime sprees of John Dillinger and other outlaws of that decade.

The seeds of the crimewave that would come in the early '30s can be traced to the end of the previous decade. Over the course of a fatal few days in October of 1929, the booming U.S. stock market experienced $26 billion dollars in losses—about a third of the total value of the market. The Crash, at it came to be known, was certainly the symbolic endpoint for the Roaring Twenties, and it ushered in a newly somber, less carefree national mood.

Despite the rebounding of the stock market, there was a fundamental weakness at the heart of the economy, one that did not come out of the blue. Despite the perception of the '20s as a time of prosperity, unemployment had stubbornly hovered around 10% for much of the decade. In part due to America's post-war economic isolationism, the agricultural sector had for a number of years been in steady decline. This was critical: though the country was becoming increasingly urban, a large percentage of the population's livelihood was still connected to farming. Finally, a substantial national debt incurred during World War I was an ongoing drag on the economy.

By the end of 1930, the reality of the Depression was undeniable. Business failures were up sharply, and GNP was down 12%. The all-important "durable goods" sector was hit especially hard—with the steel industry alone experiencing a 38% drop in production. Even with all this bad news, the numbers weren't as bad as they'd been during the brief but brutal recession of 1921, and Americans still held out hope that it was all just part of a cyclical downturn that would soon reverse itself.

It was a sudden spike in bank failures at the end of 1930 that made it all too clear that the economic downturn was not a temporary one and would likely only get worse. Throughout history, Americans had been instinctively distrustful of the idea of a national bank, and despite the creation of the Federal Reserve in 1913, the nation's banking system was still loosely regulated and prone to erratic ups and downs. Even through the supposed prosperity of the 1920s, there were over 500 bank failures every year, and during the final two months of 1930 alone, 600 banks closed their doors. These closures triggered a banking panic that would be an ongoing feature of the first years of the Depression. Worried about losing their life savings, customers would initiate a "run" on a bank, and these sudden withdrawals would force the bank to liquidate its own assets by calling in loans and selling other holdings, setting in motion a chain reaction that had the net result of drying up essential capital.

As a result of all this public unrest, the nation's banks—while hardly the only source of economic trouble—became the most visible image of the Great Depression and what was wrong with the economy. On both a practical and a symbolic level, they were a tempting target for men like John Dillinger. And because of the public's deep-seated hostility toward banks, it was inevitable that the men who robbed them would be seen by some as folk heroes.

Chapter 2: Johnnie Dillinger

As with most of the other famous criminals of the era, it is not always easy to separate myth from reality in telling the story of John Dillinger. A major part of the narrative of Depression-era "outlaws" is that, in contrast to the "gangsters" of the 20s like Al Capone, they were country boys from America's heartland. For that very reason, some early versions of Dillinger's story portray him as a country boy from Mooresville, Indiana, even though his formative years were spent in the city and in prison.

It was Dillinger's father, John W. Dillinger, who was an authentic country boy, spending all of his first 23 years on various Indiana farms. In 1887 he married his wife, Mollie, a farmer's daughter from a nearby town. But sometime in the next two or three years, John Sr., along with his wife and baby girl Audrey, was forced to move to the city of Indianapolis to support his young family. For the next decade he worked various jobs as a manual laborer, gradually saving a bit of money, and in 1900 he invested his savings in a small grocery in the Oak Hill neighborhood of the city. He would run the store for the next 20 years, never moving outside a radius of a few blocks.

John Jr., known to most friends and family as Johnnie throughout his life, was born three years after his father opened the grocery store. By all accounts Johnnie had a perfectly normal childhood in respectable middle-class household. The only significant crisis of his childhood was the early loss of his mother, who fell ill shortly after giving birth to him and died three years later.

Some early chroniclers of Dillinger's life (most notably John Toland, whose *The Dillinger Days* was for many years the definite biography) purport to find in Dillinger's childhood early signs of his later criminal persona. They claim he had a chilly relationship with his stepmother and was involved in a youth gang called the Dirty Dozen. According to other accounts, Johnnie was a petty thief as a teen and was accused of being a bully with a "bewildering personality".

However, later biographers such as Elliott Gorn find the evidence for these stories spotty at best. Extensive interviews with family and neighbors paint a picture of an unremarkable boy who got into the occasional skirmish but was reasonable well behaved. By all outward appearances, nothing seemed to suggest the making of a future Public Enemy, though he did have the kind of charisma from an early age that would be on full display during his later criminal career. John Sr. described his son as having an unusual degree of "wit", "verve" and "self-reliance."[1]

As the nation geared up for World War I, work as a manual laborer was abundant and paid well. After eighth grade, Dillinger dropped out of school and worked various jobs, including as a machinist, for the next few years. Aside from an occasional extended leave of absence, the future outlaw seems to have been a reasonably good worker.

If the loss of his mother was the first significant disruption in Johnnie's young life, the family's move to the country in early 1920 was the second. Nearing 60 years of age, and with his children entering their young adult years, John Sr. decided to return to his rural roots. He sold his grocery store and bought a small farm outside his second wife's hometown of Mooresville, where he and his new wife joined the local Quaker congregation and soon became every bit as respectable a family in the country as they'd been in the city.

Johnnie was 17 at the time, but he never quite adjusted to farm life. He suffered from hay fever and felt more at home in the nearby town of Martinsville, and he even traveled frequently back to Indianapolis to stay with his older sister Audrey. Dillinger did date a local farm girl, but the girl's father prevented the young couple from marrying. Dillinger apparently took this turn of events badly; and eventually he stole a car from a church parking lot and drove it to Indianapolis. The police found him, but in the first of many escapes Johnnie gave them the slip and ran to

---

[1] Gorn, *Dillinger's Wild Ride*, p. 7

enroll in the Navy.[2]

Johnnie's first stint as a country boy had lasted less than half a year.

Chapter 3: Young Lester Gillis

Lester Joseph Gillis was born on December 6, 1908 in a back alley flat on California Avenue on the south side of Chicago. He was the seventh child of Josef and Mary Gillis, Belgians who had immigrated to Chicago from Nova Scotia but found not so much a land of opportunity as a dark, smelly neighborhood where the sun was never quite strong enough to completely drive away the shadow of local smokestacks. Josef worked more than 70 hours a week as a packer at the Union Stockyards, while Mary cared for Lester and his six older siblings and helping make ends meet by tutoring school children in French. Delicate and devout, she believed the best about most people, especially her children, but while she and Josef worked, their sons would roam the streets around the stockyard getting into petty mischief.

While Lester's older brothers soon outgrew their childhood shenanigans, Lester was different. For one thing, he regularly skipped school, until it reached the point that teachers expected him to be absent more than they expected him to be in class, and Lester dropped out entirely after the eighth grade. Perhaps part of the problem was his size. At 5'4," Lester was often the victim of bullies and miscreants who teased him about both his size and his innocent babyface. Of course, they also found it good fun to try to scar up that face with hits and cuts.

Before long, Lester had had all he could take. One day he came out swinging and learned that he felt better when he hit back. Over the next few months he gained a reputation for being more trouble than he was worth, and soon enough even the neighborhood "toughs" who were bigger than him would cross the street when they saw him coming.

Josef and Mary tried to intervened, first with a talking, then with yelling and eventually with a razor strap. The local parish priest and the nuns who taught him at school also tried through encouragement and prayer to correct the tough little boy. However, it soon became apparent that there was something going on with Lester that went beyond the abilities of the local clergy or those of anyone else in the neighborhood either.

Soon Gillis was roaming the backstreets just looking for trouble. The Deering Street police knew that if a window was randomly smashed or a store front graffittied, it was likely the work of young Lester, as well as his friend Jack Perkins. The same theory applied to everything from stolen apples to pinched pocket knives. At first, they tried to scold the boys and talk to their parents, but it soon became apparent that that was not going to be enough to deter the growing delinquent. Perkins would later state that since Gillis was the smallest member of their group of

---

[2] Gorn, *Dillinger's Wild Ride*, p. 9

petty thieves, he usually was the kid who got the attention at the store counter and diverted the notice of the clerk while the other boys committed the thefts. In hindsight, it might be that Gillis tried to overcompensate for his perceived physical shortcomings by acting tougher and acting out even more wildly.

Lester's worst early crime was an accident. On July 4, 1921, while watching some Independence Day festivities with friends, he pulled out a pistol he'd found around town, probably thrown away by an escaping felon. The boys gathered around to look at it and Gillis accidentally pulled the trigger, shooting one of his friends in the jaw. Though the boy recovered, he was permanently maimed and Gillis was sent to the state reformatory for a year.

In 1920, at the age of 12, Gillis stole his first car. He continued with auto theft until the following year, when he was caught, arrested and convicted, receiving a sentence of a year in the local juvenile hall. As soon as he got out, he stole another car, got caught again, and was sentenced to 18 month in jail. When the teenager was away this time, Josef committed suicide. Concerned that his life of crime had driven his father to take his life, Gillis began sending money home to his mother every chance he got.

Due to some violent incidents between him and the other boys, Gillis was not released from juvenile hall until almost two years later. By then he had learned all the tricks to the criminal trade and went immediately back to the streets, robbing and pillaging small time grocery stores and local department stores. It only took five months for him to be arrested again, this time for breaking into a department store. Caught in the act, Gillis was sent to the Chicago Boys Home, a dark, creepy building with more troubled boys than the small staff could begin to handle.

Chapter 4: Dillinger's First Stint in Jail

The Navy gave Dillinger shelter from the police after he concocted a story about being from St. Louis, but he didn't fit in there any better than he had on the farm. He made it successfully through basic training, but shortly after being transferred to a ship in Boston in October, he failed to return from shore leave and was declared AWOL. He returned on his own, only to be fined and put in solitary confinement for 10 days, but the punishment didn't correct his behavior. He got in trouble shortly thereafter and was again put in solitary. In December he left for good after being dishonorably discharged from the Navy. Dillinger returned to Mooresville, claiming the Navy had discharged him for a heart murmur.

Back at home, Dillinger fell in love with another local farm girl, Beryl Ethel Hovious, and in April 1924 the young couple was married. Though his wife characterized him as charming and well-mannered in later interviews, it became clear early on that the newly married Dillinger wasn't quite cut out for the quiet life. He began frequenting local pool halls, both in Mooresville and in the nearby town of Martinsville, where he seems to have first developed friendships with the kind of shady comrades who would shape the next phase of his life.

Chief amongst these was a man in his young thirties named Edward Singleton. The two men decided to engineer a modest stickup, choosing an elderly local grocer, Frank Morgan, as their target. It is impossible to ignore the coincidence that Dillinger's first victim was a man who very much resembled his own father. Moreover, Dillinger knew the man and frequently shopped in his store.

As it turned out, the first hold-up committed by America's most famous bank robber was an utter fiasco. During the stickup, Dillinger struck Morgan over the head with a pipe, and when the old man attempted to call for help, Dillinger pulled a gun on him. The gun went off accidentally, and Dillinger and his accomplice fled with $50.

Clearly new to this line of work, Dillinger mistakenly implicated himself by asking around town about the grocer's well-being even before the botched hold-up had been reported. Not surprisingly, the police soon tracked the young man down and arrested him. At the advice of his father, Dillinger made a full confession and threw himself at the mercy of the court, while Singleton, on the other hand, pled innocent and hired a lawyer. Dillinger's strategy backfired; the judge decided to make an example of him and sentenced him to 10-20 years at the Indiana State Reformatory at Pendleton.[3]

As a result, Dillinger spent most of his 20s in prison, and it was there that he became the man who would briefly but spectacularly terrorize the Midwest. 80 years later, biographers and historians still disagree as to exactly when and how Johnnie Dillinger transformed from a troubled young adult into the brazenly suave Public Enemy Number 1. Some have argued that Dillinger was bitter from the start about being unfairly singled out for harsh punishment and vowed to become an even more hardened criminal once he got out. Others have countered that the shift took place only later during his prison term.

What is clear is that Dillinger was constantly getting into trouble almost from the day he entered prison on September 16, 1924. Most of his infractions were minor, but he also hid from the guards and attempted a few early escapes. He spent a good deal of time in solitary confinement for his troubles and had his sentence increased, but he managed to maintain high spirits, as evidenced in letters written to his family. Dillinger also apparently became acquainted with like-minded men, including Charles Makley, Russell Clark, and Homer Van Meter, all of whom eventually ran with his gang. It's believed that it was Homer Van Meter who taught Dillinger the science of crime, and it's been suggested that these men actually began planning their future robberies while still in jail.

---

[3] Gorn, *Dillinger's Wild Ride*, p. 13

Homer Van Meter

1929 was a pivotal year for Dillinger. That spring, his young wife, to whom he'd only been properly married for five months, finally filed for divorce. Soon after, the parole board turned down his appeal for an early release. Later that year he was transferred to the state prison in Michigan City. The new facility was tougher than the one in Pendleton, but it appears Dillinger lobbied for the move in order to be with some friends who'd recently been transferred there. At any rate, his troubles continued, with minor infractions and a second escape attempt frequently landing him in solitary. He seems to have hit bottom in 1932, writing to his younger brother Hubert: "It seems like I can't keep out of trouble here... I guess I am just incorrigible."[4]

However, at some point in 1932 another shift seems to have taken place. Dillinger managed to stay out of trouble and began actively planning for another appeal to the parole board the following year. Some historians make a convincing case that Harry Pierpont, a fellow convict who'd been trying for years to escape, targeted Dillinger (the most likely to be paroled first) as his way out—convincing him of the wealth and adventure that could be theirs if they worked as a team to gain one another's freedom.[5] Indeed, in just a few short months, Dillinger would be instrumental in helping Pierpont break out of jail, only to have Pierpont return the favor shortly thereafter.

---

[4] Gorn, *Dillinger's Wild Ride,* p. 19
[5] Burroughs, *Public Enemies,* p. 139

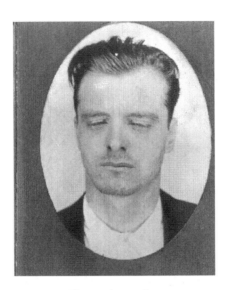

Pierpont's mugshot

Dillinger's second appearance before the parole board in early 1933 was more auspicious than his first. He had deliberately lined up the cards in his favor, getting his family to orchestrate a careful campaign that included a petition in Mooresville, and letters of support not only from his victim Frank Morgan but from the judge who had sentenced him in the first place. Other circumstances were also on Dillinger's side; with the Depression and the new crime wave wreaking havoc, prison overcrowding was becoming a serious problem.

The board ruled in Dillinger's favor, and in May he was back "home" in Mooresville. Just shy of 30 years old, Dillinger had spent nearly the entire decade of his 20s behind bar, and he returned to a vastly different world. FDR had been sworn into office just two months earlier, reminding the country that the only thing they had to fear "was fear itself", and soon after entering office the new president declared a four-day national "bank holiday" to prevent panic from spreading through the banking system. In the cities, workers were striking. In Dillinger's rural Midwest, farms fell victim to foreclosure, and the region was hit by a long-term drought that in the coming years would produce the devastation of the Dust Bowl. The nation, in short, was unsettled and uneasy.

Dillinger, in the eyes of some chroniclers, had already settled on a plan to pursue a life of crime, and in prison had forged alliances with the men who would help him do it. According to this version of events, Dillinger even went so far as to study bank-robbing, notably the innovative system devised by Herman Lamm, a German bank robber who cased his targets and used getaway drivers, lookouts, a lobby man, and a vault man. Dillinger would befriend two of the men who robbed banks with Lamm, Walter Dietrich and James "Oklahoma Jack" Clark, thereby learning about Lamm's system from men who had participated in it.

Lamm

On the other hand, some accounts at least raise the possibility that, for a time, Dillinger considered going "straight." He attended church, apologized to his victim Frank Morgan, and visited his ex-wife. Still, Dillinger had made a half-hearted attempt at being a family man 10 years earlier, but he wouldn't even really bother trying this time around. Dillinger had only 14 more months to live, and he would make every day count.

Chapter 5: Becoming Baby Face Nelson

When Gillis was released in the fall of 1926, the 18 year old thug found a whole new world of crime waiting for him. The Eighteenth Amendment to the Constitution, also known as the Volstead Act, made it illegal to produce, sell or consume alcoholic beverages. Unbeknownst to the politicians and zealous temperance advocates, the American public responded to being told that they couldn't drink by wanting to drink even more. Though Prohibition was ultimately a poorly conceived and poorly implemented disaster, it is not as simple a story as it might first appear to be. The Temperance Movement, as it was first known, dated all the way back to the 1840s, when drinking was an undeniable problem in American life. Historians estimate that per capita consumption of booze was as high as 7 gallons of pure alcohol a year, well over three times the current rate, and the equivalent of 90 bottles of 80-proof liquor a year. In response to this very real problem, groups like the Daughters of Temperance began cropping up, and later the Women's Christian Temperance Union. The Prohibition Party was founded in 1872, but it was the Anti-Saloon League, founded in 1893, that made prohibition a viable political force.

The reason Prohibition proved such a disaster was that there were plenty of underworld characters and organized crime networks fully intending to profit from it by smuggling and secretly brewing liquor. By 1926, as young Gillis was coming of age and getting into more trouble, the head of these illegal efforts to quench American thirst was reigning kingpin Al Capone, who had risen to the command of one of Chicago's most powerful mobs through brute force in the 1920s.

Scarface

According to one legend that some scholars now dispute, Gillis began working for Capone's Chicago Outfit after hearing that Capone was hiring "enforcers," thugs that would act as armed guards to keep away any cops that hadn't already been bribed into cooperation. They also knocked off the competition and protected products being moved from one location to another. Gillis jumped at a chance to get paid for bullying people, a skill he had already perfected while selling protection services to local small (and often criminal) businessmen.

As the story goes, perhaps embellished to make Gillis sound even more dangerous, Capone and his crew grew concerned with the violence Gillis used to collect overdue payments. After all, if a customer was dead, or even just seriously injured, he couldn't work enough to pay what he owed. Also, many of the underworld people he was dealing with were themselves members of the Sicilian Mafia, and Capone couldn't risk making them too mad. While they understood the need for enforcement, they were never fans of violence just for violence's sake. For those reasons, Capone's method was always to threaten rather than act when possible, but Gillis, on the other hand, preferred to hit first and talk later.

At first, Jack McGurn, Capone's lieutenant in charge of the enforcers and the man believed responsible for plotting the notorious St. Valentine's Day Massacre in 1929, tried to reason with Gillis. He explained several times that it was better to leave men afraid than maimed. Gillis, however, simply could not control himself, especially when he tasted blood. When he fought, he would often stop only when his victim was nearly dead. Unable to control him, McGurn finally had to let him go. Though furious, Gillis still had enough self-control not to cross the most powerful gangster in Chicago.

"Machine Gun" Jack McCurn

In 1928, Gillis met the only woman that he would ever love. Helen Wawzynak was working as a salesgirl in a Chicago Woolworth's when they started dating. He called her his "Million Dollar Baby From the Five and Ten Cent Store", and she was captivated by Gillis's boyish good looks and sideways smile. When they had only been dating a few months, he began to suggest they get married. However, her family was against it, and she was unable to marry without their permission because she was still just 16. Things changed a few months later when she turned up pregnant. Gillis robbed a jewelry store just outside Wheaton, put a hot ring on her finger, and used the rest of the loot to set them up in a little house in the suburbs. Their son Ronald was born in April 1930, six months after they married, and a daughter named Darlene would follow in 1932.

By the time he met his future wife, Gillis had the only respectable job he would ever hold, working for a Standard Oil Station near his home. But even then, he had a few underhanded dealings going on. He began by looking the other way while a gang of tire thieves used his station for their headquarters. Through them he met some bootleggers who hired him to haul their wares out of town to the Chicago suburbs.

One of the men Gillis worked for was Roger Touhy, a rival of Capone's and head of the infamous Touhy Gang, a mob that bootlegged liquor in the northwest suburbs of Chicago. Working with them, he quickly graduated from petty crime to armed robbery. In January 1930, the gang broke into the home of magazine executive Charles M. Richter and took more than $25,000 in jewelry. Prior to leaving, they bound him with adhesive tape and cut off his phone lines so their victim could not alert the police. After a similar robbery in March of the home of banker Lottie Brenner Von Beulow, in which they made off with $50,000 in jewels, Gillis and the others had been dubbed "The Tape Bandits".

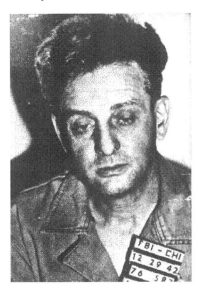

Roger Touhy

Gillis was just getting warmed up. A few months later, on April 21, 1930, he pulled his first bank job, making off with $4,000 in cash. In early October, Gillis and his cronies robbed the Itasca State Bank, making off with $4,600, and three days later, they brazenly broke into the home of Mayor Bill Thompson of Chicago and stole more than $18,000 worth of his wife's jewelry. When she described Gillis to the police, she said, "He had a baby face. He was good looking, hardly more than a boy, had dark hair and was wearing a gray topcoat and a brown felt hat, turned down brim."

Mayor "Big Bill" Thompson

No doubt flushed with their success, the Tape Bandits were back at it the following month. That November, they attempted to rob a restaurant in Summit, Illinois. This time, however, the attempt went completely haywire. It turned out that several of the patrons were themselves armed and fired on the would-be robbers, touching off a gunfight that left three bystanders dead and three others wounded. While it's unclear whether Gillis had fired any of the fatal shots in that encounter, he definitely committed murder days later on November 26, 1930, shooting and killing wealthy stockbroker Edwin R. Thompson while they robbed his home.

Despite their successful and notorious crime spree, the Tape Bandits were finally arrested in early 1931, including Gillis, who used the alias George Nelson. The press would later couple this alias with Mrs. Thompson's description, dubbing him "Baby Face Nelson" and referring to him as the leader of the group.

After he was convicted, Nelson was sentenced to a prison sentence of one to ten years in Joliet, the infamous Illinois State Penitentiary, but after he had already been imprisoned, he was charged and convicted of another crime he had previously committed, a bank robbery in

Wheaton, Illinois. This added charge brought his sentence up to possible life in prison.

Nelson, of course, had other plans. When he learned that he would be transported from his trial in Wheaton back to Joliet by train and then police car on February 17, 1932, he arranged for Helen to hide a gun for him in the train station men's room. While he may have been a little nervous about trying to take on several officers in a fully outfitted police car, he soon found out luck was on his side. Upon departing from the train, the officer in charge learned that there was no police car yet dispatched to pick them up. Rather than wait for another official vehicle, the officer simply hailed a cab and loaded his prisoner into the back seat.

All was well for a few minutes until they were well clear of the station. Then Nelson whipped out the hand gun, shoved it in the surprised cop's face and growled, "Don't give me a reason to kill you." He then ordered the driver to pull over and forced both men out of the car. With his gun still pointed at the officer's head, Nelson moved to the driver's seat and drove off, leaving the cab driver and the policeman beside the road with no way to call help.

Free once again, Nelson initially traded on his connections with the Touhy Gang to make his way to Reno, Nevada, where he hid out in the underworld then growing up around Las Vegas and went by the names Jimmy Burnett and Jimmy Burnell. He met William Graham, one of the gambling crime bosses that populated that part of the country. The two focused mostly on stealing cars, which drew the attention of law enforcement officers on the look-out for the escaped prisoner. According to those questioned, the suspect had a wife he called his "million dollar baby," as well as an infant son.

Next, he moved on to Sausalito, California, where he met John Paul Chase. Like Nelson, Chase had a reputation as a small time hood and bootlegger. The two men hit it off and were soon close friends. Chase introduced Nelson to Sicilian mobster Joe Parente, who was always looking to add another crooked limb to his criminal family tree. Before long, Nelson was doing everything from acting as a bodyguard to cracking safes and driving truckloads of liquor around the state.

Parente kept several small bungalows around Sausalito as hideouts, which allowed Nelson to move into one with Helen and baby Ronald. While they were living there, Helen gave birth to Darlene. When not robbing banks or running moonshine, he seemingly lived the life of a quiet suburban father, mowing the grass, taking the family picnicking, swimming in the ocean and sitting on the porch with his family.

While in California, Nelson made much of his living selling Parente's product to sometimes reluctant buyers. He would swagger into a speakeasy and asked to see the manager. When he came out, Nelson would inform him that he would now be serving only product supplied by Parente. If the manager took exception to this proposition, Nelson would elaborate on the sad "accidents" that had befallen others who rejected the offer. The manager would usually get the message and Nelson would usually get the credit.

However, Nelson was hardly the only tough in Sausalito playing this game. At times, when he tried to move in on another boss's territory, Nelson would find that it was his life in danger, not that of his potential customer. When this happened, he would usually contact some of Parente's other men and a battle, either literal or figurative, would ensue.

When not working for Parente, Chase and Nelson dreamed of being their own men and robbing their way into wealth and prosperity, and they shared these aspirations with their new friends, Tommy Carroll and Eddie Green. While Green and Carroll were also working for Parente at that time, they still had wonderful tales to tell of their own crime spree days, when they worked their way across the Midwest robbing small town banks as they passed through and then speeding out of town before the authorities could catch them. For a criminally ambitious man like Nelson, the small towns to the Midwest sounded like the perfect land of opportunity.

One name also stood out in many of their stories: John Dillinger. If the Midwest was the Promised Land, then Dillinger was the evil messiah for all penny ante crooks. Carroll and Green both claimed to have pulled jobs for Dillinger, and Nelson began to long to meet this legendary crime figure who had already robbed more banks than any other "public enemy" of that time.

Chapter 6: Dillinger Becomes Famous

"I'm not guilty of everything they have on me." – John Dillinger

One of the reasons it's unclear whether Dillinger tried to go straight or go straight to crime is that he may or may not have been involved in a crime spree conducted just a month after his release. According to many of the first histories of Dillinger's life, the future celebrity outlaw wasted no time in beginning his historic crime spree by robbing a bank in Ohio of $10,000. A week later, three men attempted to steal the payroll of a local thread mill in Indiana. This was followed by a series of stickups and yet another bank robbery.

Some have attributed all of these heists to Dillinger and his friends from prison, but the only evidence to back this claim is the testimony of one of Dillinger's early accomplices, William Shaw. Shaw's brief connection to Dillinger was his only link to fame, and over the years his story grew and expanded. Matt Leach, the chief of the Indiana state police, was the man who interrogated Shaw, and his accounts too show clear signs of exaggeration. Just a few months later, for example, Leach would declare to the press that Dillinger's gang had been responsible for 24 bank robberies in sixty days—a figure he seems to have pulled from thin air.[6] Given that Dillinger would be the most famous outlaw in America by the end of 1933 and his legend would only continue to grow in 1934, it's no surprise that accounts of his activity became more exaggerated over time. J. Edgar Hoover turned the Dillinger case into the crowning feather in the

---

[6] Gorn, *Dillinger's Wild Ride,* p. 42

FBI's cap, and everyone who had ever brushed elbows with the famous outlaw wanted to tell his story. Naturally, the more dramatic the details, the better the story.

But did Dillinger actually participate in these crimes? It seems far more likely that Dillinger, as his father claimed, spent those first few months looking for work, hanging around the farm, and spending time with the family. He even reportedly had a particular fondness for one of his nieces. Unfortunately, these were not good times for a newly released convict to try to go straight, with the Depression in full swing and the farm life being even harder to maintain in the Midwest. Dillinger had just spent over 9 years with ambitious criminals, and the world Dillinger knew best was the criminal network he had come to know in prison. This was his comfort zone, and in the end, that was what he fell back on.

What everyone can agree on is that Dillinger was conducting heists by the summer of 1933. On July 17, less than two months after Dillinger's release, two men robbed a bank in Daleville, Indiana, and this robbery bears many of the telltale signs of Dillinger's future heists. The men were calm and collected, and one of them nimbly leapt over the bank counter. A bank teller later identified Dillinger from a photo and described the signature scar on his upper lip.

In early August, Dillinger, his prison pal Harry Copeland, and another man hit a bank in Indiana, and a week later they hit another one in Ohio. They may have done some smaller jobs that month as well, but their biggest score came on September 3rd when they walked away with $25,000 from a bank in Indianapolis. What is striking about this initial string of robberies was the group's efficiency and organization. The robberies themselves were conducted calmly and coolly, and it was clear that the hits had been well researched and that all the necessary preparations were in place. The robbers made their getaways in stolen vehicles with recycled license plates. They were well armed, and knew whom to contact to sell items like stolen bonds. It's believed that the gang at this point consisted of Shaw and Copeland, as well as Homer Van Meter, who had been paroled four days before Dillinger from the same prison.[7]

The gang also knew where to lay low while they were between jobs. Going back to Prohibition and even before then, brothels had become an important meeting ground among the criminal underground, and it seems Dillinger made up for time lost in prison. He also picked up a regular girlfriend, Mary Longnaker, who he wrote letters to while he was out on the road.

---

[7] Gorn, *Dillinger's Wild Ride*, p. 32

Though not yet known to the general public or the press, Dillinger began appearing on the radar of various law enforcement officials and investigators in Indiana, and his parole officer began staking out the Dillinger home in Mooresville after becoming suspicious. One of the banks he had hit hired an insurance investigator who would be on Dillinger's trail for months and turn up some important leads. On top of that, Matt Leach of the Indiana State Police, his tendency to exaggerate notwithstanding, began working his contacts in the criminal world and in prison. Dillinger would quickly have all the heat he could handle.

It was the Fall of 1933 when Dillinger's budding career as an outlaw would go big-time. He had developed an extensive network of future accomplices while in prison, and not only had they been scheming together but likely were discussing which targets to hit. It's presumed that the robbers were also able to communicate with those who were still locked up. Dillinger liked these men, felt loyal to them, and shared with them a resentment toward the "system" that they felt had wronged them.

Chief among these comrades was Harry Pierpont, credited by many with being the true leader of the gang in the early days. In mid-September, Dillinger made an unsuccessful attempt to smuggle guns into the Michigan City prison where Pierpont and others were still housed. Soon after, he made another attempt, successfully packaging them in large thread spools used in the prison's work camp.

By the end of the month, Pierpont and nine others would be free men, but not before Dillinger had been captured. Acting on a tip from the insurance investigator, Dayton police had staked out Mary Longnaker's apartment. Three days after Dillinger smuggled the guns into the Michigan City prison, he himself was once more in prison. While authorities decided where Dillinger would stand trial, he remained at a relatively unfortified jail in Lima, Ohio. Early newspaper accounts of his arrest didn't even mention his name, instead referring to him by the nickname "Jackrabbit", based on his trademark leap over bank counters.

Ironically, Dillinger would become famous just as he was imprisoned. The jailbreak at Michigan City suddenly raised Dillinger's profile as newspaper accounts referred to the men as "Dillinger's Gang." It is likely that his style and charm simply made for better newspaper copy, even though at this point it appears Harry Pierpont was the clear leader of the gang. At any rate, Pierpont and the other recent escaped convicts weren't about to let Dillinger's favor go unrewarded. On the night of October 12, six men broke their friend out of the Lima jail, fatally wounding Sheriff Jess Sarber in the process while impersonating Indiana State Officers who were supposedly there to extradite Dillinger. The second local jailbreak in two weeks was big news, even warranting a mention in the *New York Times.* Dillinger had become a national figure.[8]

As if these jailbreaks weren't spectacular enough, the newly expanded gang wasted no time in moving on to an equally audacious strategy: conducting raids of local police stations to stock up on arms. Two nights after Dillinger's rescue, the group hit a station in Auburn, Indiana. A week later they hit another Indiana station and made off with a variety of weapons, including Thompson machine guns, and bulletproof vests.

Newly fortified, the gang hit a bank in Greencastle, Indiana on October 23, making away with another $25,000. In the following two days, three more local banks were hit, but those involved smaller scores and may not have been the work of the Dillinger and Pierpont gang. But that didn't stop the press, now officially in high alert mode, from jumping to conclusions. Over-the-top stories on the gang were a daily occurrence, referring to them as "desperadoes" and even "terrorists." Law enforcement officials followed suit, with the Indian governor mobilizing the National Guard and deputizing 70 new officers and 500 soldiers.

The heat was on, and Dillinger and the gang wisely laid low for a while. Using their underworld contacts, they acquired apartments for themselves and their girlfriends, largely in the North Side of Chicago. For much of November they largely stayed out of sight, spending their money and enjoying themselves.

By now, the "Dillinger gang" was so notorious that other bank robbers and underworld members wanted to be part of the gang. One young hood who was from the Midwest and wanted in was Baby Face Nelson. In 1933, things in California were getting too hot for Baby Face to continue to work there, so that May, he and the rest of his family headed to Long Beach, Indiana, where he soon hooked up with several other bank robbers, including Edward Bentz, Tommy Carroll, Earl Doyle and Homer Van Meter. Nelson hoped that Van Meter would prove to be his connection to Dillinger.

---

[8] Gorn, *Dillinger's Wild Ride,* pp. 35-42

The two men met in an Indiana bar one evening to drink and talk things over, but right from the start Nelson rubbed Van Meter the wrong way. The veteran of Michigan State Prison found the short little man with the funny nickname a joke and even told him so. Enraged, Nelson considered answering back but quickly thought better of it. Even he had more common sense than to tick off Dillinger's Number 2 man. The more Nelson tried to quote his experience and recommendations, the more Van Meter blew him off. In the end, Nelson decided that if he couldn't make it into Dillinger's famous inner circle, he'd create one for himself.

The first step toward this goal was to really learn the art of bank robbing. To do this, Nelson began putting the word out at the infamous Green Lantern Tavern in St. Paul. There he ran into Carroll and Green again, who had recently blown into town from California. No big fans of Dillinger themselves, they were glad to have Nelson and Chase team up with them, and together the four started robbing small banks across the Midwest, usually focusing their attentions on Iowa, Nebraska and Wisconsin.

Their method was always the same: burst in the doors, shoot off a couple of machine guns in the air to get everyone's attention, grab the guards and take their weapons, push all the customers and most of the employees into a corner where they could be easily watched, force another employee to open the safe, grab as much money as they quickly could, fire over everyone's heads one more time and make for the getaway car. Typically, Nelson was the first in and the last out, cursing and yelling at everyone to remove their valuables and drop them in a bag he passed around. His most notorious bank robbery during the period was an August 1933 bank robbery in Grand Haven, Michigan, which went haywire but ultimately resulted in the robbers getting away clean. As Baby Face Nelson and his gang became more sophisticated, Homer Van Meter would form a second opinion in early 1934 about letting him run with the Dillinger gang.

When things heated up in Minnesota in October of 1933, Nelson decided to take his family and his newly organized gang south to hide out. They landed in San Antonio, Texas, where the men made contact with Hyman Lebman, a well-known gunsmith who was only too happy to hook them up with new weapons to use in their future robberies. Among these was a .38 Colt fully automatic pistol that would become one of Nelson's favorite weapons.

Ironically, San Antonio soon proved to be hotter than Minnesota. On December 9, one of his neighbors called the police about a bunch of "high powered Northern gangsters". A couple of days later, two detectives, H. C. Perrin and Al Hartman moved in on Tommy Carroll, who decided to go down fighting. He killed Perrin and wounded Harman before escaping back to warn the gang. Everyone scattered, with Nelson taking his family to San Francisco, where he began a new string of robberies the following spring.

At the same time, despite the Dillinger gang's underworld contacts and their best efforts to keep a low profile, law enforcement officials were closing in. Police had their own criminal contacts, and they had developed a list of suspicious apartments that were targeted in unsuccessful raids. But the insurance investigator had managed to create a snitch by "turning" Arthur McGinnis, who had served time with Dillinger, into a paid informant. McGinnis offered to sell some of the bank bonds Dillinger and Pierpont had stolen, and in the process learned Dillinger was experiencing a skin problem and would be seeing a local dermatologist on November 15. Matt Leach mobilized a team to take down Dillinger after the doctor's appointment, but Dillinger's new girlfriend, "Billie" Frechette, seems to have tipped him off, and the two escaped.

Billie Frechette

Dillinger and the gang could have played it safe, but they decided to go for one last big score before the Holidays. They hit a bank in Racine, Wisconsin on November 20, 1933, and though they walked away with a good deal of cash, this was not exactly the smooth operation of previous heists. The head teller and at least two policemen were shot (though not fatally), and several hostages were taken as shields before being released once the gang had escaped.

The gang got away successfully, but the police were making headway. Dillinger's early accomplice Harry Copeland, not involved in the Racine heist, was arrested three days earlier. And in mid-December, John "Red" Hamilton was identified in Chicago and approached by Sergeant William Shanley. As Shanley attempted to search Hamilton, he shot the officer fatally. Shanley's murder on the streets of Chicago had suddenly raised the stakes. The city assembled its own "Dillinger Squad," and Melvin Purvis, head of the local branch of the Bureau of

Investigation (soon to be renamed the FBI) wrote his boss about the matter. Dillinger was now on J. Edgar Hoover's radar as well. Though bank robbery was still not a federal crime, the gang had transported a stolen car across state lines when they'd broken Dillinger out, and that was a federal crime.

Red Hamilton

In December most of the gang headed to Florida, arriving on the 19th at Daytona Beach, where they rented a beach house and successfully kept a low profile for the rest of the year. Back in Chicago, the Illinois attorney general declared Dillinger "Public Enemy Number One." Moreover, the rest of the top ten were all members of the gang or associates of Dillinger. Dillinger's first documented heist had been in July; in less than five months, he had emerged from obscurity to become America's most notorious outlaw. And his adventures were just beginning.

Purvis

Chapter 7: Dillinger and Baby Face Join Forces

At the start of 1934, the Dillinger gang had decided for various reasons to convene in Tucson, Arizona, a place they felt they could go undetected. But in mid-January, while most of the gang was already in Tucson, Dillinger and his girlfriend Billie made a detour in East Chicago. Dillinger later claimed he was still in Florida, but while it is understandable why he wanted to distance himself from the events of January 15, evidence indicates otherwise.[9]

Just before closing time at the First National Bank of East Chicago, two men later identified as Dillinger and Hamilton entered the bank. Dillinger pulled out a submachine gun and calmly announced, as he always did, that this was a stickup. Someone triggered an alarm; but Dillinger had encountered that before and remained unfazed. By the time all the money was bagged, the bank was surrounded by police; but that, too, was not new to Dillinger. With a police officer and a bank vice-president in front of him as a human shield, Dillinger proceeded to the door.

But what was new this time was that one of the policemen outside, William O'Malley, thought he could take Dillinger down. He yelled for the officer Dillinger was holding to duck and opened fire. The outlaw fired back. Dillinger was hit, but he was wearing a bulletproof vest and was unharmed. However, O'Malley was fatally wounded, and Dillinger's partner was also seriously hurt. The two got away, but the game had changed for Dillinger; for the first time, he was directly implicated in the killing of a police officer.

---

[9] Burroughs, *Public Enemies,* p. 188

Hamilton was treated for his wounds but would have to lay low for some time as he slowly recovered. Dillinger reconnected with Billie and the two took an indirect route to Tucson, stopping along the way to briefly visit Dillinger's father, and then in St. Louis to change cars. Eventually they reconnected with the rest of the gang in Tucson.

It would take very little time for the Feds to catch up with them. Following a timely tip from a couple who had provided the gang some assistance, along with a few untimely instances of indiscretion by members of the gang, the local police, tipped off by the Feds, had the gang's hangout staked out. On January 25, one by one, quietly and without gunfire, they arrested the gang. Dillinger and Billie were caught last. At the end of the day, the entire Dillinger gang was in jail.[10]

The news headlines were jubilant. In one fell swoop, without a shot fired, the nation's most feared gang of outlaws had been put behind bars, and Dillinger's run had seemingly come to an end. The authorities were so confident that the Chicago Dillinger Squad was reassigned to other duties. An all-star delegation of law enforcement officials from Ohio and Indiana flew to Arizona to claim jurisdiction over Dillinger—including Matt Leach, the local prosecutor, and a deputy sheriff. They arrived in Tucson to a media circus and couldn't help but get caught up in it. Dillinger had already been charming the local and providing the press with juicy quotes. He was as calm and confident as ever, but things didn't look good for him. After his arrest, the police had found among his possessions bills whose serial number could be linked to the East Chicago heist, and thus to the murder of Officer O'Malley.

While the rest of the gang was flown to Ohio to stand trial for the murder of the officer killed when Dillinger was broken out of the Lima prison, Dillinger himself was taken back to Chicago. He eventually arrived at the Crown Point prison in a 13 car convoy, where another throng of reporters awaited. Dillinger jovially posed with the prison sheriff and the prosecutor, his arm around the prosecutor—a widely circulated photo that would come back to haunt both officials.

Dillinger spent the month of February at Crown Point Prison in Indiana under heavy guard, and his trial was set for March 12. Dillinger hired a high-profile Chicago defense attorney, Louis Piquett, who was also a colorful character; a former bartender, in the early 20s he was Chicago's chief prosecutor until corruption charges forced him to step down. In private practice he represented the full spectrum of the city's organized crime scene, and on the side engaged in questionable stock market deals. His full role in Dillinger's subsequent activities wasn't clear until an unpublished manuscript telling the inside story of Dillinger's escapades was unearthed decades later.[11]

---

[10] Gorn, *Dillinger's Wild Ride,* p. 60
[11] Burroughs, *Public Enemies,* pp. 211-212

One winter day in early 1934, Baby Face Nelson heard again from Homer Van Meter. It seems that Dillinger was now duly impressed with the former two bit hoodlum and had sent Van Meter to personally invite Nelson to join their gang. Of course, it was also convenient timing for Dillinger, who had landed in jail for the third time in 1934 and had lost so many men in recent months that he was interested in merging his gang with Nelson's. Nelson agreed to the merger on one condition: he would call the shots. Much to his own surprise, Van Meter agreed.

Of course, there was still the matter of Dillinger's escape. One of the reasons Dillinger became perhaps the most famous public enemy of the era was his penchant for being captured alive and escaping alive. He had been released on parole in May 1933 after serving nearly 10 years in jail, only to be arrested 3 months later after a bank robbery and sent to jail in Lima, Ohio, where he helped plan the escape of several of his associates just days after landing there. And of course, he had been busted out of there himself in October. He had been in and out of jail seemingly every 3 months.

However, his previous escapades would be child's play compared to Dillinger's legendary escape from Crown Point Prison. On March 3, 1934, a little over a week before his trial was due to begin, the impossible happened: Dillinger, apparently without assistance, escaped from a heavily fortified prison. With just a fake wooden gun he claimed to have whittled himself and then blackened with shoe polish, Dillinger lured one guard, then another, and then another into a holding cell. With the assistance of another prisoner, Herbert Youngblood, Dillinger eventually locked up more than two dozen unarmed prison personnel, including the warden. Then, using Deputy Sheriff Ernest Blunk as a hostage, they raided the prison locker and stocked up on weapons before heading across the street to the city garage. They asked the mechanic for the fastest car, and taking both the mechanic and Blunk as hostages, they sped off, letting the hostages go once they'd put some distance between themselves and the city. Dillinger was once more a free man. Dillinger would even publicly brag about the way he escaped.

In initial newspaper accounts, and even according to many subsequent histories, this was the official story, and it fed into the legend of Dillinger as an endlessly cunning, almost invincible figure. The real story—which emerged slowly as a result of a special investigation by the Indiana attorney general and more skeptical reporters—may have been more complicated, if no less impressive. There is good reason to believe that Dillinger's attorney Louis Piquett and his right-hand man, working in concert with Dillinger's many friends in the criminal underworld, orchestrated the whole thing. Two prison employees, including the deputy sheriff Dillinger took hostage, later came under suspicion, as well as the mechanic. Their theory goes that Piquett was able to smuggle in $5,000 in bribe money, as well the wooden gun, and that Dillinger used the money to buy the cooperation of key prison personnel. But nothing was ever proven, and many both then and now prefer to believe in the initial version of the story.[12]

---

[12] Gorn, *Dillinger's Wild Ride,* pp. 70-80

Regardless of how it actually went down, Dillinger's dramatic escape had profound political consequences. Roosevelt's Attorney General Homer Cummings used the embarrassment to argue for a "New Deal on Crime" that would, among other things, expand the resources and jurisdiction of J. Edgar Hoover's Division of Investigation. Dillinger was once again a free man, but his escape set in motion a major federal effort to ensure that his freedom would be short-lived.

As was often the case with him, Dillinger wasted little time in getting back to work. For one thing, he needed money; arranging his escape had not been cheap, and those funds, not to mention other fees he owed his lawyer, had been borrowed against future earnings. The newly reformed gang gathered in St. Paul this time for a variety of reasons. St. Paul was removed from Chicago, where surveillance would be high, and it was known as a town whose cops could be bought off easily. The gang included Dillinger's old partner Red Hamilton, who had successfully recovered from wounds suffered in East Chicago, as well as Homer Van Meter, a local hood named Eddie Green, the group's driver Tommy Carroll, and Lester Gillis, better known as Baby Face Nelson.

By the time Dillinger had escaped, Baby Face Nelson had developed a name of his own, and he had previously used St. Paul as a hideout. The notoriously violent Baby Face even brought along his family to St. Paul and lived in the elegant Hotel St. Francis there between jobs. Those who encountered him would have never guessed that he was anything other than just another tourist, and he kept the local police sufficiently bribed that no one bothered them.

Things reportedly got off to a rough start when Dillinger arrived in St. Paul to officially meet Baby Face shortly after his escape. To say that the meeting did not go well would be a gross understatement. According to legend, Baby Face led off by announcing that he would be taking orders from no one, not even Dillinger himself. However, the self-confident Dillinger remained cool and continued the conversation, allowing both Nelson and Van Meter, who'd initially gone for their guns, to calm down. Even if it was technically Baby Face leading the gang, everyone outside the gang would continue to believe it was Dillinger leading things.

As if that meeting wasn't enough, the same night Dillinger arrived in town included one of Nelson's worst outbursts. Dillinger and Nelson were on their way to pick up Van Meter when Nelson, who was driving, allegedly got cut off by another driver. Enraged, Nelson began tailing the driver and forced him into a curb. Although no one was hurt, the owner of the other car, a local paint salesman named Theodore Kidder, jumped out and started yelling at Nelson. Nelson responded by pulling out his .45 and shooting Kidder right between the eyes.

But in the eyes of the press and of law enforcement, Dillinger was the key figure.

Only three days after Dillinger's daring escape, the gang hit a bank in Sioux Falls, South Dakota on March 6, 1934. As had happened before, the alarm went off, police were summoned, and a crowd gathered outside—as large as a thousand people, the *New York Times* later claimed. While Tom Carroll waited behind the wheel, the group of robbers strolled into the Security National Bank and Trust Company and shot into the air. Before anyone could blink, one of the employees hit the alarm, sending sirens screaming through the building. Nelson became hysterical and threatened to shoot everyone in the building, while Dillinger firmly ordered him back to his post as look out. Within seconds, motorcycle cop Hale Keith pulled up in front of the building. Upon seeing him, Nelson mowed him down, screaming, "I got one of 'em! I got one of the bastards! That'll teach 'em to interfere!" Though they got away with nearly $50,000, Dillinger was concerned with his uncontrollable new partner, but he realized that breaking ties with Nelson would also mean he would lose Tommy Carroll and Eddie Green, whom he needed and respected. Dillinger decided, for the moment, to keep his new group intact.

A week later they hit another bank in Mason City, Iowa, but the second heist didn't go as smoothly. Dillinger took the precaution of persuading Nelson to drive the getaway car, but things still went haywire. For one thing, the First National Bank in Mason City, Iowa had some new upgrades that Dillinger and his gang were not accustomed to. When Willis Bagley saw some suspicious looking men lurking in the bank lobby, he immediately ran into his office, taking the key to the safe with him and locking the door behind him. Though the robbers fired on the door, it remained solid and kept them out. In the meanwhile, Dillinger discovered that the bank also had a reinforced steel cage in the lobby, through which the guard on duty, Tom Walters, was able to throw tear gas into the main lobby. Eyes stinging and throats burning, the men tried to shoot through the locked cage with no success. Instead, they made their way through the smoke, cleaning out teller drawers and what money could be handed to them through the locked vault bars.

Of course, Nelson knew nothing of this, but he was beginning to get nervous standing out front for so long. By the time Dillinger emerged, John Shipley, a retired police officer working in the office across that street, had realized that something was amiss and had a sniper rifle trained on the sidewalk below. When he saw Dillinger, he fired, catching him in the elbow. Though both Dillinger and Nelson fired back, Shipley remained uninjured.

Seeing he was beaten, Dillinger dashed back into the bank and ordered the rest of the men to the car. Seeing police pulling up at both ends of the street, he also ordered them to bring hostages. As he had in similar situations in the past, Dillinger organized the bank employees into a human shield surrounding him and his men. While the police would not dare to fire, Shipley had a clear shot from his vantage point and took it, shooting through Nelson's hat and hitting Dillinger in the same arm as before. They tried to return fire, but Shipley was out of sight.

By this time Nelson was hysterical. When one of the older hostages failed to move as fast as Nelson thought he should, Nelson prepared to shoot him. However, just before he could get a shot off, Dillinger knocked his gun to the ground, saying calmly, "No need to kill him, Nelson! Now, leave these people be and do your job and get us the hell outta here — and move out easy!" Doing as he was told, the furious Nelson pulled away slowly enough that no hostages were injured. Once they were out of town, Dillinger released them. The gang was forced to leave a lot of money behind, but they had still escaped with another $52,000.

Back in the money, Dillinger took time to plan for the future. In retrospect, some have argued that Dillinger had a death wish, but many of his actions indicate otherwise. He snuck back into Chicago, met with his lawyer, and instructed him to assist his girlfriend Billie in securing a divorce from her estranged husband. He then sent Billie to Mooresville to visit his father and delivery his already legendary wooden gun for safekeeping. The couple reunited in St. Paul where they spent a couple of quiet weeks living under an assumed name.

But that quiet came to an abrupt end on the last day of March. The manager of the apartment building where they'd been staying had grown suspicious and contacted the FBI, leading two FBI agents and a local cop to the apartment to check out the tip. Billie answered the knock on the door and coolly explained that "Mr. Hellman" was out at the moment. They wanted to speak to her instead, and she bought time by asking them to wait outside while she got dressed. This bought time for Dillinger to assemble his submachine gun. In the meantime, Van Meter had arrived at the apartment building, and, sensing something amiss, he stayed downstairs with his weapon drawn. Dillinger opened fire on the agents, who, having to deal with Van Meter firing on them from below, allowed Dillinger and Billie to sneak out the back. It was another narrow escape for Dillinger and another embarrassment for the FBI.[13]

Although he had gotten away yet again, Dillinger had been hit in the leg by one of his bullets as it ricocheted off something during the gunfight. He got treatment from a doctor (who would later be imprisoned for helping him) and recuperated in an apartment Eddie Green arranged for him. J. Edgar Hoover, furious not only that Dillinger had again slipped away but that he had opened fire on two of his agents, made the outlaw the agency's top priority and put Melvin Purvis in charge of the effort. Purvis was given nearly 50 men, and together they scoured St. Paul and eventually tracked down and arrested Green's wife Bessie as she picked up some of Dillinger's things in the apartment. Though Dillinger was long gone, her arrest and questioning turned up important leads that would eventually bear fruit.

---

[13] Burroughs, *Public Enemies*, p.271

Hoover

On April 3, federal agents made their first major hit against the gang when they ambushed and killed Eddie Green. After that, the rest of the gang dispersed. Baby Face Nelson returned to Reno, where he came to the aid of two old friends, Bill Graham and Jim McKay. Graham and McKay were on trial for federal mail fraud, so Nelson kidnapped and killed the chief witness against them, Roy Fritch, tossing his dead and mutilated body down a mine shaft.

Meanwhile, in a risky move, Dillinger headed home to Mooresville for what would turn out to be one last visit with his father and family. Though he arrived at night and took other precautions, he stayed for several days, and many in town knew of his presence but chose not to share the information with authorities. During the stay, Dillinger posed for a picture that would become one of the most famous shots of the outlaw, holding his wooden gun with one hand and a submachine gun in the other as he stood in the backyard of his father's house. Why the Dillinger house wasn't already being monitored isn't exactly clear, but once again Dillinger's timing was uncanny. Shortly after he departed town, the houses of his father, sister, and brother were all raided by police. Of course, the news that Dillinger had dared to openly visit his family for a few days only added to his legend.

Dillinger with the wooden gun and submachine gun

Dillinger had eluded authorities, but the net was tightening. A week later, Dillinger and his girlfriend were in Chicago, and, as was standard procedure, Billie made inquiries about a temporary hideout for the couple. She was in a bar meeting one of Dillinger's underworld contacts while he waited safely in the car when someone tipped off the FBI, and a group of agents quickly arrived and arrested Billie. It was a breakthrough for the FBI, but also an embarrassment, since Dillinger had been there for the taking but once again slipped away.

By mid-April, the various members of the gang had come back to the Midwest. Baby Face Nelson and his wife Helen were hiding out in a cabin in Iron County, Wisconsin, and according to legend he pouted because Dillinger was Public Enemy Number One instead of him. To make matters worse, Hoover was offering a reward of $20,000 dollars for Dillinger's death, but only half that for Nelson.

Despite the heat and close calls, by the middle of that month Dillinger and Nelson felt it was safe enough to get back together and begin to plan some jobs. Accompanied by their wives and girlfriends, they checked into the isolated Little Bohemia Lodge in Wisconsin at the recommendation of Louis Piquett, who assured them it was a quiet, out of site location where Dillinger could nurse his injured arm in peace. The innkeeper, Emil Wanatka, welcomed the men as friends of a good customer, but he did not know who he was dealing with until later Friday night. That night, during a poker game, he noticed that his guests were all wearing side arms under the coats.

Little Bohemia Lodge

Wanatka mentioned this situation to his wife but decided to take a "don't ask, don't tell" attitude to his guest's identities. His wife, however, was intrigued by their glamorous and dangerous customers. The next day, she took their four year old son to a birthday party where she confided to her brother-in-law, Henry Voss, that she was nervous about having them there. He in turn informed the FBI, who sent their best team of agents, led by Purvis and Sam Cowley.

Upon arriving in Wisconsin, the more than 35 agents learned that the gang looked like they were preparing to move out. Concerned about losing their prey, they moved in quickly and without requesting back up from local law enforcement. This proved to be a mistake. First, two of the cars they were riding in broke down, forcing the agents to ride on the running boards of the remaining cars the rest of the way to the lodge. Then, unknown to them, they had come on one of the restaurant's few crowded nights, when the owner offered a popular dollar special. Seeing a 1933 Chevy coupe leaving, the agents ordered the occupants to halt. When they didn't, they thought they had their men and sprayed the car with bullets, killing innocent customer

Eugene Boisneau and wounding John Hoffman and John Morris. Morris and Hoffman would later explain that they never heard the order because they had the car radio on.

At that moment, gang member Pat Reilly pulled up with his girlfriend, Pat Cherrington. Seeing the agents, they managed to escape in the confusion. Likewise, Dillinger, Van Meter, Carroll and Hamilton went out the back door, which the FBI officers had failed to secure. After moving through the woods on foot, the four split up, stole a couple of cars and drove off into the night, leaving Nelson to face the cops alone.

This predicament didn't seem to bother Baby Face. Coming out of his cabin shooting, he exchanged fire with several agents before making his way into the lodge. There he made his way out the back door, just as his partners had, but he took off in the opposite direction. When he finally made his way out of the dense woods, he was about a mile from the lodge and at the home of a couple named Lange, whom he kidnapped and ordered to drive him away. When Mr. Lange didn't drive fast enough to suit him, Nelson ordered him to pull over so that he could drive. Whether Lange meant to or not, he pulled up in front of the home of local switchboard operator Alvin Koerner, who had already heard about what was going on and called authorities to tell them that he had one of the gangsters in his front yard.

Just as Koerner hung up, Nelson burst through the door and ordered Koerner to freeze. Moments later, the innkeeper Wanatka and two other men arrived at the house to check on Koerner. Nelson also took them hostage. Unbeknownst to him, however, a fourth man had remained hidden in the back seat of their car. Nelson ordered Wanatka and Koerner into the car, not noticing the fourth man in the back seat. Wanatka took the wheel and prepared to drive off, but before he could put the car in gear, two federal agents and a local constable arrived. Not realizing what they were getting themselves into, they let Baby Face get the drop on them. He ordered them from their car but then opened fire, killing Agent Carter Baum and wounding Agent Jay Newman and Constable Carl Christensen.

With the agents out of the way, Nelson jumped into their car and sped off, but even now he wasn't in the clear. Before he could get far a tire blew out and the car became stuck in the mud. Unable to get to the tire to change it, Nelson took off on foot through the woods and came upon the cabin of a Native American family, whom he stayed with for several days before stealing their car and driving off.

Much to Nelson's dismay, Helen and two other women were captured by the FBI at the lodge. Though they questioned all three extensively, they could find no evidence of any serious wrongdoing on anyone's part. After charging them with harboring fugitives from the law, the police released them on parole, probably hoping that the women would lead them back to the fugitives.

In total, the incident at Little Bohemia left one agent and one innocent citizen dead, two agents and two citizens wounded, and the Dillinger gang unscathed. Needless to say, the public was not happy. Some were calling for Hoover to resign, while others insisted the agent Purvis, who headed up the fiasco, be fired. To deflect criticism from himself and his team, Hoover emphasized to the public the sacrifice of the brave, heroic Agent Baum, who had given his life protecting theirs, and reassured everyone that he would not rest until Baum's killer was brought to justice.[14]

The gang had slipped by the FBI at Little Bohemia in several groups and that was how they escaped. Dillinger, Hamilton and Van Meter stole a car from another nearby lodge and made their way back to St. Paul. They circled around the town and came in from the south, thinking that would be safer, but local police recognized the reported license plate and gave pursuit. A gunfight broke out and Hamilton was mortally wounded, but Dillinger and Van Meter escaped to Aurora, Illinois.

Dillinger was out of sight for much of the next two months. He and Van Meter engaged in a relatively small heist on May 2 just outside of Toledo which netted $17,000, more than enough to tide them over for a while. For weeks they lived in an abandoned shack outside of East Chicago, and then they lived in their truck, sleeping on a mattress in the back by night and driving the backroads by day.

It was on those Indiana back roads that they made their second noteworthy public appearance in May. In an incident on May 24 about which there are wildly conflicting reports, their truck was approached by two plainclothes East Chicago detectives. With Dillinger at the wheel, Van Meter opened fire at the men and killed them both. Subsequent accounts suggest the two detectives may have been set up by a fellow officer, Martin Zarkovich. Zarkovich, who had repeatedly fallen under suspicion for corruption, had also been seen at the Crown Point prison while Dillinger was there. The theory goes that he had some involvement in Dillinger's breakout and wanted the detectives, who knew about ongoing bribing of the East Chicago force, eliminated.[15]

Regardless, Dillinger and Van Meter knew they had to get off the roads after that, and they eventually settled down for most of the month of June in a seedy apartment on the far North Side owned by an associate of Dillinger's lawyer. There they came up with a plan to disappear even more completely. Dillinger had for a while entertained the notion of disguising himself through plastic surgery. He finally prevailed upon his lawyer to hook him up with a couple of doctors of questionable character who agreed for a fee of $5,000 to conduct the surgery, first for him, then for Van Meter. The operation wasn't exactly a success. Their crude methods of anesthesia nearly killed Dillinger, and even after a long bloody operation, the outlaw was still mostly recognizable despite the removal of several moles, a building up of the nose, and a filling in of his chin

---

[14] Burroughs, *Public Enemies,* Chapter 12
[15] Gorn, *Dillinger's Wild Ride,* pp. 131-132

dimple. And despite the issues with Dillinger's operation, Van Meter went ahead with his own operation. The two men also had their fingerprints removed.[16]

In spite of the absence of real news about Dillinger over these two months, America's Public Enemy Number One hardly disappeared from the news. If anything, Dillinger's low profile only added to his legend. An endless stream of articles appeared on the FBI's debacle at Little Bohemia, and Dillinger "sightings" came in from around the country. At the end of June, Dillinger celebrated his 31st birthday, and though his surgery scars were still healing, he actually began spending time in public. He attended baseball games at Wrigley Field during the day and went to clubs at night. With his previous girl Billie having been convicted the month before, he even found a new girlfriend, Polly Hamilton.

While Van Meter remained more cautious, the plastic surgery apparently emboldened Dillinger and gave him hope that he was still invincible. As in the Hollywood movies that his life sometimes seemed to resemble, Dillinger dreamed of one last big score, after which he would ride off into the sunset and disappear for good in Mexico, Latin America or some other exotic locale. On June 30, Nelson, Dillinger and Van Meter held up the Merchants National Bank in South Bend, Indiana. Helping them may have been another Public Enemy, Pretty Boy Floyd, although that has never been proven conclusively. Regardless, the robbery began badly and only got worse. Van Meter immediately shot and killed the first police officer on the scene, Howard Wagner. Then Nelson was fired on by a local jeweler, Harry Berg, who hit him in the chest. However, Nelson's bulletproof vest kept him from being seriously injured, and their exchange of shots wounded an innocent bystander. In the ensuing chaos, an unarmed teenaged boy named Joseph Pawlowski tackled Van Meter, who hit him over the head with his gun.

Meanwhile, Dillinger and his accomplices ran out of the bank carrying about $28,000 and bringing along three hostages. Undeterred by dangers to the civilians, the police still fired, wounding two of the hostages and grazing Van Meter's head. Though several other citizens were wounded in the melee, the police did accomplish what they set out to do: neither Dillinger nor Nelson would ever rob another bank.

Tired of being away from the city's nightlife, Dillinger moved from the seedy apartment at the edge of town to an apartment run by Anna Sage, a former prostitute who now had her own brothel and had in fact introduced Dillinger to his new girlfriend. Dillinger and Polly lived it up over the next few weeks, and Dillinger's extreme confidence and risk-taking seem to have been rooted in a plan he and Van Meter were brainstorming. They had been developing a plan to ambush and rob a mail train. Using nitroglycerine, they would blow open the train's armored car and walk away with their biggest score ever. The plan so captured their imagination, they even began talking about writing a screenplay detailing their exploits.[17]

---

[16] Burroughs, *Public Enemies,* Chapter 14
[17] Gorn, *Dillinger's Wild Ride,* p.141

The line between reality and the movies was blurring. And in an entirely fitting way, that theme of unreality marked Dillinger's end. Even while he and Van Meter were plotting their grand plan, a plot to bring the famous outlaw down was falling into place. Anna Sage was facing serious legal troubles. She was a Romanian immigrant facing deportation by the U.S. Immigration Service, as well as new prostitution charges. She brokered a deal with the Feds, mediated by none other than Martin Zarkovich, the corrupt East Chicago cop who also happened to be her boyfriend. She told the Feds that she was going to the movies with Dillinger and Polly Hamilton the next night, and that she would be wearing an orange dress so that the authorities could spot her. Though she was unsure which theater they were going to, she told them it would either be the Biograph Theater or the Marbro.

On the night of July 22, Sage accompanied Dillinger and his girlfriend to the movies. Ironically, the film they attended was *Manhattan Melodrama*, the story of a gangster played by Clark Gable who ends up going to the electric chair for his life of crime. Meanwhile, the Feds were waiting outside both the Biograph Theater and the Marbro Theater, so conspicuous that the Biograph's manager actually called the Chicago police on them, thinking they were criminals casing the place. When the Chicago police arrived, the Feds had to wave them away.

Led by Melvin Purvis, the agents waited outside the theater, having decided it would be best to take Dillinger down as he left the film. As the film ended and customers came out, Purvis signaled Dillinger's exit by lighting his cigar while standing at the entrance. Somehow, Dillinger got the sense that something was wrong; after making eye contact with Purvis, Dillinger stepped out ahead of the two women and tried but failed to grab his gun. As agents approached him and ordered him to surrender, Dillinger tried to flee into an alley, only to find that federal agents had closed that escape off. At least three agents fired several rounds at Dillinger, hitting Dillinger in the back and sending him face first to the pavement. Dillinger had been hit three or four times, with the fatal shot having gone through the back of his neck and out his head just below his right eye, killing him instantly. The man credited with firing the fatal shot, Charles Winstead, would be given a personal letter of commendation from Hoover himself.

The apparently invincible outlaw Houdini who had slipped away so many times had finally met his end.[18]

---

[18] Gorn, *Dillinger's Wild Ride,* pp. 142-145

The Biograph Theater in 1934

Dillinger's legend only grew with his death, and the myth-making began almost from the moment his body hit the sidewalk. A huge crowd gathered that night, scavenging for souvenirs and hoping for a glimpse of the dead outlaw. As people around the theater began to realize what had just happened and who the target was, some of them dipped their handkerchief in the famous outlaw's blood. Crowds followed Dillinger as his body made its way, first to the hospital where he was declared dead, then to the coroner's office, and finally to a funeral home in Mooresville. Rumors began circulating about a "lady in red" who had betrayed Dillinger. The coroner's office returned a mere seven dollars to Dillinger's father, and another set of rumors grew about what had happened to all of the outlaw's money. Still more rumors flew around about Dillinger's brain having been removed during the autopsy.

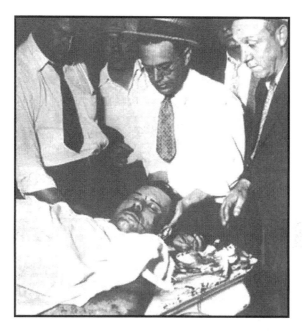

Dillinger's body

Of course, like Jesse James and other famous outlaws, rumors that Dillinger had somehow escaped or not been killed outside the theater persisted. Author Jay Nash has extensively argued in his book, *The Dillinger Dossier*, that the man killed outside the Biograph Theater that night was not Dillinger but another petty thief known as Jimmy Lawrence, who slightly resembled Dillinger. Nash's theory was that Martin Zarkovich set up the elaborate plot to have someone take the fall in Dillinger's place, which would allow Dillinger to escape the heat, and that the FBI covered it up upon realizing that they had killed someone other than Dillinger. According to his elaborate conspiracy, Nash insisted Dillinger was still alive and well, living out his life doing manual labor in California.

J. Edgar Hoover carefully nurtured his official version of the Dillinger story. Shortly after the outlaw's death, Van Meter and Nelson and other famous Depression-era bandits were captured or killed, lending credence to Hoover's claim that the new federal War on Crime was bearing fruit and reversing the tide. The following year, his Division of Investigation was renamed the FBI, and the hunt for Dillinger was front and center in the new agency's own history of itself. In his office, Hoover installed an exhibit case holding an array of Dillinger memorabilia, including the hat and glasses the outlaw was wearing the night he was killed. Up to this day, FBI trainees engaged in target practice sometimes shoot at life-sized John Dillinger targets. Over the years,

Hoover carefully turned the outlaw into a symbol of his agency's triumph and a moral lesson that crime does not pay.[19]

Chapter 8: The Battle of Barrington

With the most famous outlaw of them all now dead, Pretty Boy Floyd became Public Enemy Number One on July 23. Then, Van Meter was killed in St. Paul, Minnesota by police a few weeks later, leaving Nelson the sole survivor of the original gang. Floyd was killed the following October, putting Baby Face in his much coveted Public Enemy Number One Position. By this time, the Nelsons and Chase had gone back out west, moving from place to place in California and Nevada. They then returned to Chicago in November, moving into the Lake Como Inn in Lake Geneva, Wisconsin.

Nelson might have lived on had he stayed in hiding, but it was clear that he and Dillinger simply could not stand inactivity for long periods of time. Instead, he began to make noises around town about looking for some new men to help him start another bank robbing enterprise. By now, however, he found no one was interested in working for him. His reputation as a loose cannon preceded him, and even the most hardened criminals were reluctant to get involved with a man who had a tendency to shoot it out with cops than slip away quietly with the loot.

By November 1934, Cowley and Purvis were trying to track Nelson's every move and were closing in on him. They knew that he was somewhere in the Chicago area and were determined to find him. In order to do so, they had as many men as they could assign patrolling all the major highways outside the city, traveling up and down the road looking for Nelson, whom they were all trained to recognize.

On November 27, 1934, their hard work finally paid off. Federal agents William Ryan and Thomas McDade caught up with Nelson, Chase and Helen in front of a gas station just north of Chicago. As it turned out, Nelson had also been doing his homework; he had compiled a list of license plates used by police and federal agents, which allowed him to recognize cars and even try to attack them. Thus, when Agents Ryan and McDade recognized Nelson while driving the other way down the road, he also recognized them as agents. Both cars did U-turns to try to chase each other, and in a strange twist of fate, it was Nelson who started chasing the agents.

During the chase, the agents exchanged fire with Nelson and Chase, whose shots had shattered the agents' windshields. For their part, the agents radioed to their bosses and Ryan fired a shot that destroyed the radiator of Nelson's Ford. Just as bullets rendered the agents' car useless, Sam Cowley and Herman Hollis picked up the trail.

---

[19] Powers, *G-Men*, pp. 114-115

FBI's photograph of Agent Hollis, who was credited with firing the fatal shot that killed Pretty Boy Floyd a month earlier

Due to the damage inflicted by the agents on Nelson's car, he swerved the car into the entrance of Barrington's North Side Park as Hollis and Cowley went driving past him. As the outlaws fired at the federal agents and Helen ran for an open field to escape, Hollis and Cowley slid their car in nearby and took cover behind it. Expecting a gun battle with each car acting as a fortress, the agents were shocked to see Nelson walking toward them, firing his .351 rifle so many times in succession that bystanders would later incorrectly believe he had a machine gun. As Nelson exposed himself, the agents hit him multiple times with submachine gun fire. However, Chase was still firing from the protection of the outlaws' car, and Nelson somehow summoned the strength to sit up on the running board of the car and keep pumping shots at the agents, eventually mortally wounding Cowley while Hollis's shotgun blasted him in the legs. Even still, Nelson kept getting up, and as he did so Hollis tried to move behind a utility pole, only to catch a bullet in the head.

With Hollis all but dead and Cowley mortally wounded, Nelson somehow staggered to his feet and made his way to the agents' now bullet-riddled car. Chase hurried over and got behind the wheel, and the two scooped up Helen and fled the scene. Hollis was dead on arrival, and Cowley would die the next day after unsuccessful surgery.

The fact that Nelson was still alive as the outlaws fled was miraculous; he had been shot 17 times, with seven submachine gun bullets hitting him in the chest and 10 shotgun pellets ripping into his legs. Chase drove them to a safe house in Wilmette, Illinois, but as Nelson told his wife,

"I'm done for." He died in bed at the safehouse that same evening. Chase would eventually be apprehended and sent to Alcatraz.

A local newspaper gave a rather terse description of the battle, emphasizing the importance of the officers, rather than the criminals.

"Special Agent Samuel Cowley and Special Agent Herman Hollis were shot and killed by the infamous gangster Baby Face Nelson near Barrington, Illinois.

When two other agents had encountered Baby Face Nelson, his wife, Helen Gillis, and a male companion, John Paul Chase, driving down a road, a gun battle ensued as both parties recognized each other. The agent's, with their windshields shattered, were forced off the road into a field but not before they had disabled the suspect's car.

As Agents Hollis and Cowley approached the scene and exited their car, they were met with gunfire by both male suspects. Agent Hollis, with massive head wounds, was pronounced dead upon arrival at a hospital and Agent Cowley died the following morning after surgery for his stomach wounds.

The suspects fled the scene in the agent's car and drove to a house in Wilmette. Baby Face Nelson, who had been shot nine times, died there later that evening. His body was discovered wrapped in a blanket in a ditch in front of a cemetery in Skokie. He had also been responsible for the murder of Special Agent W. Carter Baum seven months earlier."

A few weeks later, after Helen Gillis had been taken into custody, the *New York Times* sent a reporter to her sister's home, where they received a different take on the events of that day.

"Mrs. Fitzsimmons reveled to newspaper men that Mrs. Nelson had told her that she, Nelson and the other man were in a cottage near Lake Geneva, Wisconsin, for ten days until a raid by Federal men a week ago yesterday, when they fled out the back door and escaped in a car.

On the way to Chicago, she related, they sped safely through one Federal trap, in which several shots were fired, and then raced on to encounter Cowley and Hollis near Barrington.

'The Federal men's fire disabled our automobile,' Mrs. Fitzsimmons quoted the widow as saying. 'I could almost feel the bullets as they whistled past my face.'

Following that, Nelson, the unidentified man and Mrs. Nelson leaped from the car.

'Les hollered at me to duck and I jumped into a ditch and kept my head down,' the widow was quoted as saying. 'I could see Les firing back at the Federal men who were trying to kill him.'

'A few seconds after the firing started I could see Led jump up and grab his side. I seemed to know that it was over. I was in that ditch until the firing stopped.'

She said the three fugitives climbed into the Federal car. Nelson attempted to drive, but was too weak, and the other man took the wheel, Mrs. Nelson said to her sister-in-law.

She said they found their way to a house "somewhere near Chicago," into which they carried Nelson, stripped him of his clothing and attempted to care for his machine gun wounds.

'All three of us knew Les was dying,' the widow was quoted as saying. Later, she said, he told her to say good-bye for him to their two children.

At 7:35 that evening, three hours after the battle, she said, Nelson died, and they took the body to a point near Niles Center.

'We placed his body on the grass,' Mrs. Nelson was quoted as saying. 'I covered him with a blanket and tucked it around him because he always hated the cold weather.'"

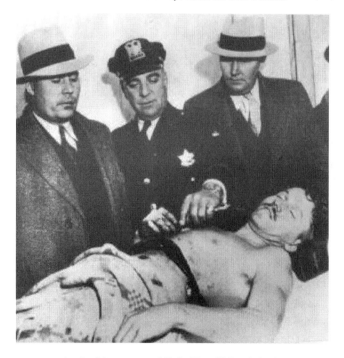

Authorities surround Baby Face Nelson's body

Today Baby Face Nelson remains yet another name on a short list of criminals who rose to fame during the Thirties. While he aspired to be like the handsome, dashing John Dillinger, he was simply too volatile to emulate Dillinger or capture the public's attention in the same way as his cool, calm, and collected partner. While his wife certainly grieved for him, as did his two young children and John Chase, most of the rest of his underworld associates breathed a sigh of relief when he was gone. While they respected Dillinger for his calm, well thought-out planning and relatively less violent demeanor, they despised Nelson's flamboyance and cockiness. No matter how many times he was told, he could never understand that his love of unnecessary violence brought too much attention to other criminals who were just out to make a buck.

Of course, it seems obvious now that making money was never at the heart of what Nelson did. In his mind, making a name for himself, trying to get respect to make up for those who had tormented him as a child, was always more important. In that sense, he got what he wanted. By running with Dillinger and being Public Enemy Number One himself, America has not forgotten Baby Face Nelson. And if anything, the glamorization of his contemporaries, from gangsters like Al Capone to outlaws like Dillinger and Bonnie & Clyde, have allowed Baby Face Nelson to be lumped in by association with those who were more captivating and level-headed.

Chapter 9: The Dillinger Gang's Impact

If Dillinger's life often seemed to resemble a Hollywood movie, Hollywood went on to play a major role in his ongoing legacy. The movie industry underwent a profound shift in the early '30s. Films that openly romanticized flashy urban gangsters like Al Capone had been a mainstay of Hollywood in the '20s, but in response to public fear and revulsion of crime in the Depression, the industry imposed on itself a strict code that would remain in place for two decades, one that banned glorification of violence and sex. For a brief period of a couple of years, however, explicit violence was allowed if the purpose of the film was to denounce criminality and extol the virtues of law enforcement.

During this transitional period, the public got their fill of movie violence in films that romanticized not criminals but those who sought to put them behind bars, particularly the agents of the newly revitalized FBI. Emblematic of this shift was the actor James Cagney, who appeared as a gangster in the 1932 film *Public Enemies*, only to reappear as a federal agent in the 1935 film *G-Men* (short for "Government Men," popular slang designating FBI agents).

As the Hollywood Code of the '30s eventually fell into disrepute and became outdated, movies exploring the grit and grime of criminal life began reappearing. Gangster films started making a comeback in the '50s, and Dillinger himself has naturally popped up in every decade. Some of his more notable appearances include Warren Oates in the title role of a 1973 film, Robert Conrad in 1979's *The Lady in Red*, and Johnny Depp in Michael Mann's 2009 *Public Enemies*.

Dillinger has remained a pop culture fixture since his spree and demise, but his life and death had an important impact on the real world as well. The wave of bank robberies for which the '30s were famous was most heavily concentrated in the struggling farm states of the Midwest, and J. Edgar Hoover would go so far as to call the tri-state area comprising Kansas, Missouri and Oklahoma the "crime corridor." As early as 1930, a bank raid in this region was a weekly occurrence, more often than not followed by a car chase.

As urban banks fortified themselves with updated security measures, bandits turned toward more vulnerable rural banks. In addition to featuring less formidable security, rural banks allowed outlaws to quickly disappear into the countryside via a vast network of newly paved roads. While bank robbers such as Dillinger might have been embraced as folk heroes by some, this was not the case among the rural townspeople of the Midwest. As more and more banks in the region fell victim to well-organized heists, locals began forming "citizen protective associations" to supplement bank security. Informal posses sometimes sped off in pursuit of fleeing getaway cars, often at great personal risk.[20] Dillinger's gang had come across vigilantes on a handful of occasions, and his success ensured that such a system stayed in place.

In recent years, some historians contend that the crime wave of the early '30s was more a product of perception than of reality.[21] What these historians argue is with society apparently crumbling around them, the American public saw outlaws like John Dillinger, and the spectacular crimes they committed, in highly symbolic terms. As one historian puts it, "every major crime was turned into a test of whether America and its values could survive the depression."[22] Amidst such a fearful environment, the federal government actively encouraged this perception, in a sense "marketing" outlaws and promoting them as celebrities. They did so to justify the passage of an ambitious package of anti-crime legislation that radically redefined the role of the federal government in law enforcement. The War on Crime that emerged from this legislation served two purposes. First, it reassured an anxious public desperate for a semblance of order and normalcy. Second, it paved the way for aggressive federal intervention in other areas of American life as well.

A look at the historical record provides some evidence for this view. The FBI didn't collect national crime statistics until 1930, and even then the records were sketchy until 1933. But examinations of crime trends in various cities suggest that "serious crime in America rose to a peak in 1918 and steadily declined until the 1940s."[23]

But if the actual crime wave of the 1930s was a subjective matter, the public reaction to that perceived crime wave was all too real. After the Lindbergh kidnapping in 1932, an editorial in the *New York Herald Tribune* declared that an "army of desperate criminals which has been recruited in the last decade is winning its battle against society." Other papers calls for citizen

---

[20] Potter, *War on Crime*, pp. 69-72
[21] among others: Claire Bond Potter, *War on Crime;* and Richard Powers, *G-Men*
[22] Powers, *G-Men*, p. xv
[23] Powers, *G-Men*, p.295

vigilante groups, an American version of Scotland Yard, even nationalization of the police. The first use of the term "Public Enemy" to describe a criminal was by the Chicago Crime Commission, a private gathering of lawyers, bankers, and businessmen that had gone as far as hiring its own investigators to seek punishment for high-profile criminals. The public, and the culture, were demanding action. The popular "Dick Tracy" cartoon strip pre-dated the actual War on Crime by several years. When Attorney General Homer Cummings finally assembled his national Conference on Crime, it was a belated response to a swelling of public opinion long in the making.[24]

Much has been made of the contrast between the urban gangsters of the 20s and the rural outlaws of the 30s. There were indeed some real differences; Al Capone and other gangsters of the Roaring Twenties saw themselves as businessmen trying, in their own way, to become part of and take advantage of the system—a system that was viewed by many as offering everyone a real the chance of prosperity. By contrast, John Dillinger and other Depression-era outlaws saw themselves as enemies of the system at a time when that system seemed to be failing the majority. But the contrast between outlaws and gangsters can be overdrawn. Dillinger and other outlaws spent considerable time in jail before embarking on their crime sprees, and while in prison they came into contact with established figures of organized crime who would prove to be key allies once they were released. In between their notorious bank heists, outlaws needed a place to lay low, and they frequently made use of the brothels and clubs controlled by organized crime.[25] They also used their underworld contacts to obtain weapons and to get rid of stolen goods. It is no accident that the supposed farm boy John Dillinger spent his final days and met his end on the streets of Chicago.

Bibliography

Burroughs, Bryan. *Public Enemies.* New York: The Penguin Press, 2004

Borus, Daniel H. (ed.) These United States — Portraits of America From the 1920s . Ithaca, NY: Cornell University Press, 1992.

Cromie, Ronert and Pinkston, Joseph. Dillinger: A Short And Violent Life. Chicago Historical Bookworks, 1962.

Gorn, Elliott J. *Dillinger's Wild Ride.* New York: Oxford University Press, 2009

Kennedy, David. *Freedom From Fear.* New York: Oxford University Press, 2001

Lindberg, Richard. Return to the Scene of the Crime. Nashville, TN: Cumberland House, 1999.

---

[24] Powers, *G-Men,* Chapter 2
[25] Potter, *War on Crime,* p. 86

Nash, Jay Robert. Bloodletters and Badmen. NY: M. Evans & Company, Inc., 1995.

Nickel, Steven; William J. Helmer. Baby Face Nelson: Portrait of a Public Enemy. Cumberland House Publishing, 2002.

Potter, Claire Bond. *War on Crime.* New Brunswick: Rutgers University Press, 1998

Powers, Richard Gid. *G-Men.* Carbondale & Edwardsville: Southern Illinois University Press, 1983

Wallis, Michael Pretty Boy. NY: St. Martin's Press, 1992.

William, J. Helmer. Baby Face Nelson. Cumberland House, 2002.

Zion, Sidney. Loyalty and Betrayal — The Story of the American Mob. San Francisco: Collins Publishers, 1994.

Made in the USA
Lexington, KY
08 July 2014